Between Two Countries

Between Two Countries

CHELSEA FAGAN

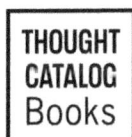

THOUGHT
CATALOG
Books

BROOKLYN, NY

THOUGHT
CATALOG
Books

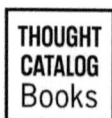

Published by Thought Catalog Books, a publishing house owned by The Thought & Expression Co., Williamsburg, Brooklyn.

Second edition, 2018

CONTENTS

Introduction

The night before I moved to France, I couldn't eat anything at the nice dinner my parents had taken me out to for our goodbyes. I was so nervous, so completely unsure that leaving everything behind was a good idea. Vacations were easy, and spending a few weeks at a time in France had given me just enough desire to move there permanently without ever really thinking about what that meant. Signing up for a school, getting a job, buying my tickets, securing my visa—it was all painting a picture that I couldn't really see clearly until the eve of my departure.

But it was, without a doubt, the greatest choice I've ever made. It was an emotional cliff-dive, taking an enormous risk in the hope there would be a payoff, and there was. Every bit of my life changed for the better, though often not in the ways I had imagined they would. Taking enough of a gamble to move to a new country is something that changes you, that leaves you with much less hesitation over the many other opportunities that will come your way thereafter.

Every time a friend told me that I was "lucky" to be moving to a new country, I told them that they could each do it, too. Every time they told me that having French as a second language was a gift, I reminded them that it was a gift everyone could give themselves. Living in another country does not have to be an extended, trust-funded vacation through a culture you will never understand. Being bilingual is not something that only genetic lottery can decide. Traveling, immigration, and settling into a new country are all things that we can each do if we decide how much it is worth to us.

In compiling this book, I wanted to draw from the pieces of my experience that are at once unique to France and universal to those who leave their home countries. I want to paint a picture that isn't the millionth macaron-and-baguette version of an American living in Paris. We deserve to learn from one another, to be a sponge instead of a rock, and the first step to all of it is getting on that plane you've always been dreaming about.

Bon voyage.

1

What Happens When You Live Abroad

A very dependable feature of people who live abroad is finding them huddled together in bars and restaurants, talking not just about their homelands, but about the experience of leaving. And strangely enough, these groups of ex-pats aren't necessarily all from the same home countries, often the mere experience of trading lands and cultures is enough to link them together and build the foundations of a friendship. I knew a decent amount of ex pats — of varying lengths of stay — back in America, and it's reassuring to see that here in Europe, the "foreigner" bars are just as prevalent and filled with the same warm, nostalgic chatter.

But one thing that undoubtedly exists between all of us, something that lingers unspoken at all of our gatherings, is fear. There is a palpable fear to living in a new country, and though it is more acute in the first months, even year, of your stay, it never completely evaporates as time goes on. It simply changes. The anxiousness that was once concentrated on how you're going to make new friends, adjust, and master the nuances of the language has become the repeated question "What am I missing?" As you settle into your new life and country, as time passes and becomes less a question of how long you've been here and more one of how long you've been gone, you realize that life back home has gone on without you. People have grown up, they've moved, they've married, they've become completely different people — and so have you.

It's hard to deny that the act of living in another country, in another language, fundamentally changes you. Different parts of your personality sort of float to the top, and you take on qualities, mannerisms, and opinions that define the new people around you. And there's nothing wrong with that; it's often part of the reason you left in the first place. You wanted to evolve, to change something, to put yourself in an uncomfortable new situation that would force you to into a new phase of your life.

So many of us, when we leave our home countries, want to escape ourselves. We build up enormous webs of people, of bars and coffee shops, of arguments and exes and the same five places over and over again, from which we feel we can't break free. There are just too many bridges that have been burned, or love that has turned sour and ugly, or restaurants at which you've eaten everything on the menu at least ten times — the only way to escape and to wipe your slate clean is to go somewhere where no one knows who you were, and no one is going to ask. And while it's enormously refreshing and exhilarating to feel like you can be anyone you want to be and come without the baggage of your past, you realize just how much of "you" was based more on geographic location than anything else.

Walking streets alone and eating dinner at tables for one — maybe with a book, maybe not — you're left alone for hours, days on end with nothing but your own thoughts. You start talking to yourself, asking yourself questions and answering them, and taking in the day's activities with a slowness and an appreciation that you've never before even attempted. Even just going to the grocery store — when in an exciting new place, when all by yourself, when in a new language — is a thrilling activity. And having to start from zero and rebuild everything, having to re-learn how to live and carry out every day activities like a child, fundamentally alters you. Yes, the country and its people will have their own effect on who you are and what you think, but few things are more profound than just starting over with the basics and relying on yourself to build a life again. I have yet to meet a person who I didn't find calmed by the experience. There is a certain amount of comfort and confidence that you gain with yourself when you go to this new place and start all over again, and a knowledge that — come what may in the rest of your life — you were capable of taking that leap and landing softly at least once.

But there are the fears. And yes, life has gone on without you. And the longer you stay in your new home, the more profound those changes will become. Holidays, birthdays, weddings — every event that you miss suddenly becomes a tick mark on an endless ream of paper. One day, you simply look back and realize that so much has happened in your absence, that so much has changed. You find it harder and harder to start conversations with people who used to be some of your best friends, and in-jokes become increasingly foreign — you have become an outsider. There are those who stay so long that they can never go back. We all meet the ex-pat who has been in his new home for 30 years and who seems to have almost replaced the missed years spent back in his homeland with full, passionate immersion into his new country. Yes, technically they are immigrants. Technically their birth certificate would place them in a different part of the world. But it's undeniable that whatever life they left back home, they could never pick up all the pieces to. That old person is gone, and you realize that every day, you come a tiny bit closer to becoming that person yourself — even if you don't want to.

So you look at your life, and the two countries that hold it, and realize that you are now two distinct people. As much as your countries represent and fulfill different parts of you and what you enjoy about life, as much as you have formed unbreakable bonds with people you love in both places, as much as you feel truly at home in either one, so you are divided in two. For the rest of your life, or at least it feels this way, you will spend your time in one naggingly longing for the other, and waiting until you can get back for at least a few weeks and dive back into the person you were back there. It takes so much to carve out a new life for yourself somewhere new, and it can't die simply because you've moved over a few time zones. The people that took you into their country and became your new family, they aren't going to mean any less to you when you're far away.

When you live abroad, you realize that, no matter where you are, you will always be an ex-pat. There will always be a part of you that is far away from its home and is lying dormant until it can breathe and live in full color back in the country where it belongs. To live in a new place is a beautiful, thrilling thing, and it can show you that you can be whoever you want — on your own terms. It can give you the gift of freedom, of new beginnings, of curiosity and excitement. But to start over, to get on that plane, doesn't come without a price. You cannot be in two places at once, and from now on, you will always lay awake on certain nights and think of all the things you're missing out on back home.

2

Where You Will Find Yourself

One day, my friend told me that she was moving to South America because she felt like, whatever she was meant to become, she wasn't going to become it here. (Here was Washington, DC, and for what it's worth, I feel like DC seems pretty big and "discovery-ready" for many people. It was for me at the time, anyway.) There's always a certain air of pretentiousness, of privilege, surrounding blanket statements like that. We were having coffee in a city I had long dreamed of coming to, and she couldn't wait to shed it off of her like a molting snake. I suddenly felt embarrassed over being so excited about DC, like it was only a stepping stone when she was moving onto The Real Thing.

She came back two years later. She was tanner, and thinner, and had longer hair. From what I could tell, though, she was pretty much the same. She seemed content, and to have found what she was looking for. As long as she got something out of it, that's what matters.

We are told to look for ourselves, and the things that we are supposed to do as though we are going to find them under a certain rock on a certain street in a certain city. There are people who spend years traveling around, uprooting themselves any time they feel their heels digging into the dirt, looking for a fresh start to appease the sense of itchy restlessness that accompanies a stagnant zip code. Aside from the initial questions about financial logistics that a life of wandering conjures, one wonders what can really be constructed when you are constantly saving up for your next ticket out. "Go find yourself" is an appealing question only when you have the means and the time to be constantly looking.

One can hope to find a safety net, I think. If you find the ability to stretch out in all directions and make mistakes and meet new people, I think you've found something exciting. On my first birthday upon arriving in France, I'd only been here for a few weeks. I thought I would be spending it alone, maybe going to dinner with one friend if I was lucky. As it turned out, a half-dozen of the people I had known from my previous visit to the city had gotten together to celebrate with me in some of their favorite bars they wanted to show me. Some of them even brought gifts. I think I cried that night. I'd never felt so lucky, so safe. It became apparent that what was most important to me when I was going across the world to find myself was to find people who cared about me, to find a home, just like the one I already had. If you can find that sense of home in a new place, maybe you can start to find yourself.

But we are everywhere. Even though we left every city we used to be in, we were there, too. And even the places you were the most exhausted with in the moment are transformed into something nostalgic, even magical, when you get enough distance on it. You see the same people, the same bars, the same streets long enough, and all you want to do is get away to "find" yourself somewhere new. But you leave, and then you think about those friends and those bars and they all seem so wonderful — maybe because they belonged to a different version of "you" that you weren't even aware you had.

It is so important to take those moments every day to stop, breathe slowly, and look around at what you have. Because even if you want to get on the next plane out of the country to find a better future, there is something significant around you right now. You are finding yourself in this restaurant, in that park, in this crappy little apartment. You are finding yourself in the wrong person's bed after a long night. You are finding yourself waiting for the metro on the same route you've taken to work for the past seven months. And even if it takes moments of significant beauty — like those people who got together to make my first birthday here special — to make us notice it, we are always living it. There is always a part of us which is growing, which is learning something new, which is taking something for granted.

I asked my friend what she found in South America. "A lot of stuff," she said. "But I kind of missed DC sometimes." I think the city missed her, too. She needed to go and find something, and it's good that she went, but she'll never be the precise person she was when we knew each other in DC again. I hope the person that she found in South America was better, and more mature, and ready to learn even more things about life. But I hope that person — the one she became — is able to understand that the person she used to be was just wonderful the way she was, too.

3

The Beauty Of Learning
Another Language

In a certain way, the learning of a new language is always a love story. Though its applications are often much more functional than they are romantic, the discovery of something so rich and complex — something which contained and created such a vast history before you even thought to seek it out — always comes with an element of infatuation. There is something profoundly humbling about staring before a vast expanse of words and phrases and sounds that insist on taking shape slowly, methodically, and only for the most patient touch. The thrilling gains and frustrating plateaus of navigating a linguistic landscape which was not made with you in mind, while often driving us to the brink of exasperation over our own abilities, constantly remind us that there are near-endless other worlds out there to be explored.

There are, of course, the first toddler-like steps you take when you fumble through words and sentence structures with all of the grace and nuance of a bull in a china shop. You mash your words together, you hesitate and stutter through even your most simple phrases — the act of putting together a coherent thought seems too daunting to ever be a realistic possibility. But with language we seek out, there is always that love, that heady thrill that comes with collecting little morsels of knowledge about this vast new tapestry of communication. It could be the culture of the speakers you have fallen for, or the language's literature, or simply the way the sounds roll from deep in the back of the throat and bounce off the tip of the tongue. You might enjoy the soft, rich tones of French or the elegant, rhythmic cadence of Japanese. There might be just a haunting depth to the words being spoken in that language which, for you, extends far beyond the content of what is being said.

And this love pushes you through frustrating hours of rote study that can feel more stilted than arithmetic and more futile than holding wind in your hands. Running a constant obstacle course, you conduct your first conversations and start to feel as though the language you are speaking is no longer simply memorized sounds being grasped from thin air. The sounds begin to take forms that follow one another, that make sense, that form coherent stories and thoughts and expressions — the small bits you retain come along with their context, part of a greater whole that you are beginning to understand. There is a shape forming around you, and though you cannot fully identify its lines or curves, you are aware that it is present — that it provides the backdrop of everything you are beginning to use yourself. The sounds around you start to build to a kind of frenzied crescendo of understanding, bombarding you with meanings and histories that you are now starting to put into neat little categories, egging you on to take the essential next step.

So you immerse yourself. You go to a place where you can

marinate fully in not just the sounds and songs and the idiomatic expressions, but the people and the colors and smells and everything that makes the language something less tangible than a set of characters written out in a certain order. The sound of the language falls around you like heavy, warm blankets, telling you over and over that you are learning, making even the most mundane exchanges profoundly interesting. Every day, every second, provides a new opportunity to trip and stumble into a new level of understanding, of pronunciation, of fluid ability to express oneself.

Your first dream in your new language wakes you up with a kind of conviction in your ability to learn that is rarely experienced. The brain seems almost to have run away with the knowledge you have fed into it, to have taken it and molded it into something that can no longer be fully expressed in speech. The language has taken root in you and expanded throughout every corner of your subconscious, unfurling and wrapping itself around concepts that you once considered unique to your mother tongue. To think, to feel, to make jokes in this new language feels almost a privilege, something that must be tended to and expanded so as not to rest on some sophomoric plateau of half-understanding.

But learning becomes more fluid now, less an active seeking out of information and more a gradual taking in of all that's around you. True, there remains as much as ever to learn about the second language, but now that you can see it through the better-adapted prism of itself, the concepts and grammatical structures and slang become parts of a whole you have already constructed and are now coloring in. You have swam upstream, and now you can bathe in the calmer waters of unintentional learning.

Every word becomes a gift. Every stone is upturned to reveal a new way of thinking that seems to not exist in your maternal language. The responses that you now have to certain things seem tempered, if not fully colored, by a new culture and phrasing through which to process it. The snowball seems to roll ever-faster downhill, collecting more nuance than you ever considered possible when you embarked on the journey, when you learned your first pronouns. The expressions that once seemed isolated in a cloud of guttural sounds and glottal stops have now become fully-formed aspects of daily life. You are no longer learning a language, you are simply living in it. Many people may doubt your accent, ask where you come from, or even assume you are a native speaker. Your grasp on the spoken word no longer seems even in the realm of the secondary, it seems something you have innately. You are, as we have come to call it, fluent.

There will come moments when you trip over your own tongue which, in some ways, will always remain a tourist to these words. You may stumble and see yourself in the more unflattering mirror of a visitor who hasn't quite figured everything out. The vast expanses of shared cultural history and references that will always to some degree elude you begin to seem like a horizon past which you cannot see. But to have climbed that mountain and, more importantly, to have realized that the top of this mountain is just another flat, everyday piece of land to a whole other world of native speakers — that can never be replaced.

4

10 Reasons To Travel This Year

1. If you don't take the first step, you'll never do it.

It's so easy to get stuck in this cycle of "I'm going to go — I can't go right now — I'll go next year — I'm going to go," and never get out of it. There is, after all, a lot of logistics that go into getting out there and seeing the places you've always wanted to see. If you're looking for one, there is always an excuse not to get those tickets. But the second you take the plunge and decide that you're actually going (and making the painful-but-necessary financial investments to do so), everything else has a tendency to fall into place.

2. It's less expensive than you think.

While the purchases of things like tickets are always going to sting a bit, there are so many ways to make your travels feasible to do on the cheap. If a hostel is too pricey for you (though there are many which offer beds at 15 bucks a night or even less in major cities), couch surfing is a wonderful option. If you don't know anyone, check any of the many websites which organize couch surfers. (Speaking personally, I and almost all of my friends in Paris have hosted couch surfers at one time or another, because we understand that it's a city so many people want to see at some point, and we don't always have a ton of disposable income to do so.) It's actually incredibly fun for hosts to meet new people and be able to see their city through new eyes. They can also help you eat cheap, local food and shop places where you won't be another ripped-off tourist. It's win-win, and practically free. (Of course, it's always encouraged that you buy a meal or bottle of wine for your host, and help with chores when possible — but still, that's nothing compared to a hotel.)

3. You don't ever have to be alone.

Whether you meet people in your hostel, stay on someone's couch, or join an online travel group before you go which organizes meetups for people passing through the city, there is never a reason to be alone while traveling if you don't want to. Being young and in a new city is one of the easiest ways to meet tons of people, and gives you a million things to talk about in every conversation with a stranger. It's a time you don't have to be afraid of first impressions, or the baggage of your life back home. Everything and everyone is a clean slate, and you can meet as many people as you want on your journey.

4. But you can be alone if you want.

If you are more interested in spending some alone time, however, there are a million ways to go about that. You can just leave for a day and go wander around a new city, taking everything in and being at peace with your own thoughts. You can take pictures or sit down in cafes and write about everything you see, and don't have to be on anyone's schedule. It's rare that we get these kind of moments back home, and we owe it to ourselves to have them once in a while, if it's what we want.

5. Plane travel is an adventure in itself.

Just the act of getting in a plane and feeling it take off, or navigating the byzantine chaos of an airport in early morning, can be a thrilling experience that we easily forget we can have. There is something terribly frightening but also wonderfully life-affirming about the moments before takeoff, or the glimpses of patchwork fields you can get from over the wing. Even the often-disappointing selection of airplane food becomes something wonderful and exotic when you're going somewhere you've been dreaming about for years. It's a moment that means you got out, that you overcame the false starts, and that something new is waiting for you.

6. Once you get there, moving around is easier.

Take, for example, Europe. You come primarily to see Rome, but you want to get around and see other things. Between cheap train tickets with the 12-30 discount cards, incredibly cheap airlines that hop between European cities, and car shares that are easily accessible online and can cross entire countries in a few hours, there are limitless ways to get from one place to another once you've already taken the leap across the ocean. Whichever continent you're headed to, though, you'll find that (in many ways thanks to the internet) the means of shorter travel to make the most out of a single trip are growing exponentially every day.

7. You never know what will happen when you get there.

It's so cliché, but it's said often for a reason. You can spend years rationalizing how you aren't missing that much by not going, or how you don't want to risk not having a good time, or that you won't know what to do when you get there, but the truth is you have no point of reference. The amount of incredible things that you could happen on your trip is literally unimaginable. You can say that you don't need to see it, but you really have no way of knowing exactly what you're missing out on.

8. You will invariably learn something about yourself.

It can be as simple as, "I can navigate a foreign city by myself and get around with a language book full of only useful phrases. I can use my limited skills to get good food, accommodations, and meet new friends." Even this is an incredibly important and affirming thing to know about oneself, and the only way to learn it is to get out and see what happens when you try.

9. It's good to get out.

No matter how much you love your current place of residence, it's just all-around a good thing to get out every now and again and see some new surroundings. You are able to put some comparison up against the corner bars you are used to, the restaurants you frequent, the architecture you're surrounded by, and the public transportation you use every day. While you may end up finding that you prefer where you came from, it's nice to see just how much of our own cities we take for granted as being universal, and even how the buzz of a city around dusk can feel completely different in a climate which is almost identical. Cities have their own lives and personalities, and we sometimes forget that ours is far from being the only kind out there.

10. There are so many people you haven't met yet.

Maybe you won't meet the love of your life waiting to cross a street in a foreign city. Maybe you won't have a whirlwind two weeks with them where you explore your new environment and learn the first fumbling steps of a new language. Maybe you won't end up remembering this city for the rest of your life as the place where everything wonderful first began. But maybe you will, and that's reason enough to go.

5

The Difference Between Alone And Lonely

Alone is calm. It's being somewhere with nothing other than your own thoughts, able to hear the things that you often intentionally block out with meaningless conversations and loud music and well-attended parties. Alone is listening to the things you have to say to yourself, giving time to the more important reflections that you often allow to settle in the back of your mind like a fine dust swept under a rug.

Lonely is talking to yourself to the point that you are sick of your own voice inside your head, the nails-on-a-chalkboard sound of your own echo chamber — your thoughts and your thoughts alone, reaffirming themselves over and over until almost nothing has any meaning left. It is wanting a sounding board for all of the things you've discovered on your own, the things you want to confirm with the comforting reality of hearing another human being speak them aloud.

Alone is eating dinner for one, taking the time to savor each dish instead of having its flavor interrupt you as you try to carry on your conversation. It is reading a book in the corner,

3

undisturbed by everything else going on around you, happy to exist in a scene where the only partner one needs is the soft din of conversation around you.

Lonely is seeing this scene, this dinner for one at a table in the corner, as a reality that has become too routine to see as special. It is wanting to talk about how good the food is, how professional the service, how charming the decor — and having no one in particular to give their opinion in return. It is leaving a review on a website so you have someone to share the experience with, because you don't want to feel as though yet another meal has served little purpose other than to give you momentary nourishment.

Alone is taking a break from the pressures of your social circle, happy to stay at home for a while and simply recharge. It is ordering food, choosing a movie that you've been wanting to see forever, and cuddling up with as many pillows as you want to take for yourself. It is feeling the satisfaction of selfishness, the refreshing reprieve from having to take others' concerns into account. It is being as informal and messy as you want to be, happy in the knowledge that no one will be there to judge you if you don't get to the dishes right after you finish eating.

Lonely is allowing this freedom from judgment to take root in your life, to become a reason to let things go. It is dishes piling up in the sink, a bed going unmade for days, the same greasy meal being ordered from the same takeout place every night for an entire week. It is losing perspective of other people to the point that your entire world narrows down to you and exactly what you're doing in that moment.

Alone is walking along a street, just you and your city, taking things in that you often don't take the time to appreciate when you're busy with other people. It is allowing your senses to be your company, talking to you with a million different voices of how good this smells or how wonderful that feels. It is taking the time to soak in your surroundings, instead of just existing blindly within them.

Lonely is seeing something so beautiful that you feel your heart cannot contain it all by itself, that it is going to burst from the radiance that it is longing to express. It is wanting to turn to someone, anyone, and say "Look at that. Isn't that wonderful?" and realizing that, as with so many other memories of late, there is just no one there to share it with.

6

Stop Delaying That Big Trip. Stop It.

As anyone who moves to another country knows, one of the guaranteed side effects of your change in time zone is going to be your friends, acquaintances, and even strangers constantly telling you how "lucky" you were to "get away." Of course the initial reaction can be a touch of resentment at the implication that your arriving in this new land was simply a result of falling into an airplane/ pile of money, and waking up magically in the apartment of your dreams. As we know, it's most often through a lot of hard, tedious work, patience, mountains of bureaucracy, and being at the bottom rung of everything for a while until you get adjusted to your new culture, language, and space. But for people who dream of living somewhere else—people who have a need to explore, learn a new language, or have always dreamed of a particular city, there is nothing more rewarding. And while when you're boarding the plane with no return ticket and no clear idea of how you're going to suddenly construct an entirely new life for yourself, things can be incredibly intimidating, no drug on the planet could possibly replace the thrill. It's wonderful.

But even just to take a trip to a new country you've always dreamed of is an undertaking in itself—even if you plan on having firmly in hand that mythical return ticket so many of us have yet to procure. Sure, riding rickety trains from city to city in Eastern Europe, whittling your own walking stick in the Himalayas, renting a tiny bungalow on a beach in Thailand, drinking wine and eating good bread under the Eiffel Tower—these all seem amazing. They seem like some kind of dream. Yet they seem so far away. They seem somehow unattainable—that there are too many things standing between you and the foreign joy you've so long imagined. Paperwork, plane tickets, finding a place to stay, learning those cursory phrases that prove to be much more indispensable than you could have anticipated—not a one can be left off the list. Personally speaking, though I have known since I was a little girl that I always wanted to go to Paris and had learned to speak the language before setting foot in the territory—I had many false starts for my big trip. Even when I didn't plan to live there, I just wanted to visit, there was always something that stood in the way—some reason I couldn't justify it. Even when friends in Paris would offer me a place to stay, tickets were at their most inexpensive, and the weather was perfect—something happened and I didn't go. By the time I finally made my first trip, it felt like I could finally exhale after holding my breath for years. I had done it; I was here.

And now, I hear at least once a day from someone—whether here in France looking to finally see the U.S., or from friends at home who won't use my offer of a couch in my apartment to convince themselves it's time to finally see Europe—that they just "can't go." The timing isn't right, the money isn't there, they have to get a new passport, they can't find anyone to go with, they can't get vacation time, things are just not going to work out right now. And these are often the same people who've been talking for six straight years about how much they want to go and travel—they are the ones who actively want to get out. I'll have the same conversation over and over with friends—often friends who are at the peak no real responsibility/ a decent amount of disposal income combination. Friends who have jobs, sure, but have vacation time to take if they plan ahead of time. It goes like this, time after time:

Friend: Ugh, I'm so jealous of you. I want to see Europe so badly. I really should go. I want to come to Paris and drink coffee at those outdoor tables!

Me: Well, you should come and visit! I can come get you from the airport and you can stay with me!

Friend: Yeah, but the tickets are so expensive.

Me: Well, if you buy them now, they'll be about 550 bucks round trip for the early summer—which is the best time to come, I think.

Friend: Yeah, but I don't think I can get time off of work.

Me: Why don't you talk to your boss now and see what time you have available this summer, and then go off of that?

Friend: Yeah, I don't know. I'll let you know.

Cut to them not getting back to me, and them starting the next conversation with me a few weeks later with "Omg how is Paris ugh wish I were there." And this is almost universal—the exact same justifications, the exact same desire to go, the exact same reasons why it will never work. Year after year after year. And granted, I have had friends visit with me and they've always enjoyed the city and it always helps to have someone to show you around and help you figure things out, not to mention the free bed. Not everyone has talked themselves out of it. However, most of the people I've seen here from the States are people to whom traveling in general is an indispensable part of life, something that comes at the top of their leisure spending priorities. In fact, I recently had a conversation with a friend about this very topic—one who is what I would refer to as a "travel addict." He said,

I don't make that much money. I mean, I make enough, but I stay in hostels and couch surf and always live on the cheap when I travel. I buy tickets way in advance for off-season times and I try to find places where I know people I can stay with or who can show me around. When I'm home, I don't spend a ton of money on going out or shopping for a few months before I travel—it's something you can save for if you want to. There's always a way to put the money aside, especially when you're young and don't have a family or a house or whatever. Anyway, if I don't do it now, I probably never will—I couldn't live with that.

And yet, when people talk to him, they consistently act amazed that he manages to get around the way he does without his parents' help or a very lucrative job. He is equally bewildered, I think, with how much they don't realize they spend just going out at night or shopping on weekends. To each his own, of course, but to act as though traveling—especially when you're young—is some kind of insane luxury that is utterly unattainable unless the stars align perfectly and God hands you a couple hundred dollar bills while no one is looking is ludicrous.

My best friend here in Paris works in the hotel industry, and loves his job. He is the ultimate guide—you tell him someone is new in town, he'll introduce them to everyone and show them the five best places to go for any occasion. He knows where to get the best croissant—which is different from the place with the best pain au chocolate, it must be said. You imagine he just has a map of the city on the palm of his hand that he checks when no one is looking. And when you ask him about his favorite thing about his job, he'll say,

When a much older couple comes in, and they can't do much in their day, so you have to help them find the best things for what they like that aren't too far apart. They'll say, "Thank you so much. We've been waiting all our lives to take this trip—but it just got so hard to come here with children and the house and everything. We just didn't come." Nothing makes me happier than making their trip special and exciting. And they'll always say, "You're so young. Go see the world, then come back and build your life."

7

Why Everyone Should Go To Paris At Least Once

I have lived in Paris for nearly three years, the home of my second language and my second family that first made me miss my own just a little bit less, and I am soon leaving. I am moving to New York with a French man and three suitcases and an incredibly heavy heart. It's for the best, I know, but that has never been a sentiment which takes the sting off of a tough decision. I've been to New York a few times, never for very long, and even in its ubiquity, it feels incredibly unfamiliar and intimidating. Where Paris has always been a collection of neighborhoods, nearly completely unmarred by the distant loom of a skyscraper, New York is a real city. It is loud and tall and bursting with limitless energy. When I walk along the river at night here, alone except for the people singing in my headphones, I realize how the peace that I have come to love even in a city so large is something not granted to most metropolises.

When I look out of the big double windows of my perfect-for-me little St Michel apartment, I wonder if I will ever be able to carve out such an understandable slice of life for myself again.

I have managed to tame and master one city, but it was a soft one. I don't have many callouses from the process.

I very rarely write about Paris, even on my personal blog or with my friends from back in the States when we exchange long catch-up emails. And it's mostly because I feel, quite simply, that there is enough written about Paris as it stands. There has never been a shortage of eager, curious, existentially hungry Americans who've gone to the City of Light to find themselves and ended up writing essays or books of all lengths to describe the way they feel looking into the reflection of a tiny cup of espresso on a bright, clear Paris fall morning.

And it's always struck me that there is a narrative that exists about Paris, one where the people are haughty smokers and the cafés are busy and the parks are incredibly well-manicured. And part of this is true, to be sure. But it seems significant that so many of the people writing about this city — even those who live in it for years — write about it with the perspective of a particularly impressionable visitor touring some kind of theme park. They don't speak much French, and even if part of their story is comprised of the hilarious foibles involved with learning to conjugate irregular verbs when confronted with an impatient pharmacist, their involvement is always conditional.

They speak to Parisians on English terms, a change in dynamic which is bound to render nearly interaction just a bit less natural than it would have been otherwise. And I love fish-out-of-water tales, but we have enough of them when it comes to Paris. I'd like to start hearing more from, say, Barcelona, if anyone has good recommendations for some travel reading.

But one of the things that has always made me love Paris so deeply is how much it transcends cliché, how little of it really falls into that perfectly charming narrative about existential ennui and cheap red wine. While there is nothing more sensually fulfilling than spending a day shopping in old Parisian speciality shops, filling up your basket with cheese and bread and reveling in the realization that some things are popular for a reason, it comprises such a small slice of life here that it's as much a novelty to its inhabitants as it is to someone watching Amélie for the first time.

Most nights out change the bottle of wine for a couple of good mojitos or a pint of Belgian beer. Most shopping trips involve swinging by the Monoprix on the way home from work and hoping that you didn't get there past the time when they stop selling alcohol. Most morning coffee happens either at your kitchen counter, passing briefly through a bakery, or stopping by a Starbucks. There isn't a whole lot of time to just linger, unless you're in one of those devastatingly fashionable neighborhoods whose lunch hours magically last all day.

When I first came here, I was working as an au pair. When you work in such a position, the entire culture of "French luxury" stays as foreign to you as it was before your plane landed. You take the metro early, you take the baby to the park and to school with the other nannies, you stay late helping to clean up after dinner. You live in a small room, and get paid a negligible stipend. You walk through the posh shopping districts, pining after a purse that would take four months' worth of your salary to buy. You see the people in their smart blazers and Inès de la Fressange skinny jeans, and you recognize that they belong to another world. You are just one of the cogs that makes the machine turn, and makes it look so effortlessly good.

Paris is beautiful, but it's always more beautiful for someone else.

And even as a writer, when my occupation and geographical

location matched up for a mental image of the most superficially fulfilling life one could imagine, Paris is still just a normal city. The architectural backdrop and culinary underpinnings are thrilling to the senses, but even those get dulled after a while. Just as in any city, it is the locals who are least likely to take in the monuments, stroll through a museum, or seek out the most aesthetically pleasing parks. It's almost cynical how numb we can become to the immense beauty that surrounds us. The daily grind of grocery stores and post offices and pharmacies and paperwork become as much of a distraction as they do anywhere.

And that is precisely why I always encourage people to come here when I can. Because it is important for us to realize, when we actually set foot and grow accustomed to a place about which we have dreamed for so long, that nothing can ever live up to our porcelain expectations. Nothing will ever be a one-dimensional narrative of espresso and baguettes and striped shirts. And that is what makes life most beautiful, most engaging, most surprising. To have your expectations wiped away from your eyes and be left with the reality of a city of 2.5 million people, and to understand that it is still something worth dreaming about, is all the confirmation we need to appreciate what we have when we have it. I will miss the simple trips to the grocer or to my friend's apartment or to my favorite neighborhood bar the most, not Montmartre or the Jardin de Luxembourg (even though they are beautiful).

That is a life we can carve out anywhere, that is the simple beauty that rises to the top like cream, even in a city as rich in everything as Paris.

You should come to Paris because you will be, in some way, disappointed by it, as we are with any image we have built up in our heads for so long (as I was the very first time I came here, after so many years spent looking at my postcards and my books and my charming French movies). And in your disappointment, you will realize that there is something much more beautiful under the Haussmanian rooftops and the narrow, winding sidestreets. You will realize that there are real humans here, people whose lives carry on unbeknownst to us, who cannot translate themselves into a rough idiomatic equivalent in English, and whose world will always remain just a little bit of a mystery to us. And you will realize that this — not the monuments — is really what has kept us so in love with this city for so many years.

8

The 23 Hardest Things About Moving Home After Living Abroad

1. Having dreams where you're back in your old city, in your old apartment, and everything is exactly the way it way — and then waking up and realizing that, at least for now, that chapter of your life is closed.
2. Occasionally messing up your speech patterns and using strange syntax because your brain is, in many ways, still working in the second language and you don't quite know how to change directions without throwing everything into reverse.
3. The three or four food items that — beyond just being the overall cuisine that you miss — had come to be your diet staples that you don't really know how to live without anymore.
4. Trying to plan your trip back to go visit all of your friends and realizing that airplane tickets are just as expensive as ever, if not more so.
5. Having to factor in airplane tickets into your budget

on a semi-regular basis, for pretty much the rest of your life, because you're either going to be there and visiting home or home and visiting there.

6. Trying to explain to someone who is going on a vacation to your city all the things they absolutely have to do and realizing that a) it's impossible to do all of the things that you want them to do in any reasonable frame of time and b) you're probably just confusing them with all of your overwhelming, sometimes incoherent advice.

7. Becoming incredibly jealous of anyone who is going there on vacation, because you wish so badly that you could be going (and part of you selfishly believes that they'll never appreciate it enough, or in the right way).

8. Suddenly remembering all of the "touristy" things you never took the time to do — monuments you didn't see, museums you didn't tour — because you told yourself you would get to it next month, next year, someday.

9. Having Skype sessions with people back there and wishing you could reach through the screen and give them a hug, or grab something off of their plate that you haven't gotten to eat in forever.

10. No longer living in your adopted language, where every cultural reference is a new gift to be discovered, and you pick up expressions and slang like a child finding shells along a beach.

11. Knowing that it would be selfish of you to expect all of your friends to come visit you here because transportation is so expensive, but always keeping a

spare bed or at least a sleeping bag for anytime someone makes the trip.

12. Fearing that, whether it's the language itself or the person you were there, that it's all a muscle that will atrophy if you don't constantly work it. (By the way, there is absolutely no shame in language or country-based meetups now that you're back home — in fact, they're kind of an essential part of life from now on.)

13. Worrying that you're bringing up your old country too much, even if you lived there for years, because you know that people perceive it as "pretentious" or "bragging" if you talk about the place you used to live.

14. Wishing that you could take everyone who wants to travel by the shoulders, give them a shake, and tell them that it's possible if you want to do it, and that there are so many different ways to make the logistics of it all work if you're willing to try.

15. Getting so frustrated when people tell you how "lucky" you were to live abroad, when you know intimately how much tedious paperwork, hard work, and trying in the face of rejection it actually required. You know how little of it actually has to do with luck, especially when you're actually working in your adopted country.

16. Experiencing these weird, listless times where all you want to do is listen to music and watch movies from that country so you can feel, if only for a minute, like you're back there.

17. Trying to recreate some of your favorite dishes and — even if you are successful — realizing that it's never

quite the same without the surroundings and people that go with it.

18. Eventually realizing that there just isn't enough space on your wall to fit all of the photos, maps, and prints that you want to put up from your time abroad — and that you'll kind of look like a crazy person if you do.

19. Postcards. So many postcards everywhere, from so many people.

20. Spending way too much of your hard-earned money at speciality stores that carry the stuff you simply can't live without, and hating yourself every time you drop 10 dollars on something that was 2 dollars back there.

21. Having no one to share your love of the music from your time abroad, and having everyone look at you really strangely when you put on some obscure German rap or Argentinian pop when you have a house party.

22. Occasionally slipping in an expression or word from that language, without meaning to, into an otherwise English sentence (and knowing that everyone thinks you're really pretentious for doing it, even though it was completely an accident).

23. Realizing that you're not really sure what "home" is anymore, because even though this is technically where you come from, you're not sure you fit into the shape of the puzzle piece that you left behind. In a lot of ways, your time abroad felt much more like home, and maybe you won't ever really feel settled until you can actually call it that — even if you're all too familiar with how difficult immigration is. Being

where you belong, maybe not today but someday, is something you're willing to work for.

How To Fall In Love With A New City

Arrive. Feel incredibly inadequate all of a sudden — one never realizes how much of their confidence is based on familiarity with their surroundings until they are thrust into a place where they recognize nothing. Everyone seems to dress better, to talk faster, and to make you feel as though you are a child who has suddenly been allowed entrance to the grown-up table at Thanksgiving. Everything you do seems to be a faux pas, a way of revealing yourself as the new kid in town, the tourist. You discreetly check maps and ask for help, not wanting to seem as lost as you are.

And everything is foreign. The signs don't make sense, the public transportation seems designed to throw you off, and no one is friendly. The locals seem to have this calculated cool, a certain kind of immunity to the frenetic pace of their city, to the noise and the dirt and the pushy pedestrians. Everything passes around them in a kind of hum and they remain undisturbed, crisp in their freshly dry-cleaned clothes and dignified haircuts. It's as though you have shown up for a test that only you haven't prepared for, struggling while the rest of the class breezes through the multiple choice questions.

Every now and again, though, the city itself extends a hand to you — reminds you that you're not as alone as you think you are. There are nooks and crannies everywhere willing to take you in and make you feel as though you are still love by the people around you. You find a nice coffee shop with a friendly waiter who is happy to give you directions and recommendations for a good place to dinner that night, your port in the storm of a life that won't slow down for you to adjust to. A warm, smiling face holds open a door for you, starts a small conversation waiting in line in a store. The tendrils of local life begin to reach out and wrap themselves around you, from the merchants who know your name to the neighbors who say hello in the hallway, to the familiar people in line for their morning coffee.

The city begins to take shape, to feel less an amalgam of experiences and noises and more a functional map within your mind of places and people you have a connection with. You take long walks at night, exploring small streets and allowing yourself to think only of where you want to have dinner that night. As you become familiar with geography, so you become adjusted to what it means to live here. In every city, we are different people. We allow ourselves to become infused with the people and foods and habits of our surroundings, taking on a regional charm that can't quite be recreated elsewhere. "She's from New York," someone might say, "You can tell he's from London," they'll remark. You seem almost stamped with the bar code of your zip code.

And you realize that the attitude you may have initially mistaken for harsh indifference is actually camouflage-like adaptation to your surroundings. Without realizing it, the residents melt so completely into the bakdrop of their city that they are no longer fazed by any of its petulant mood swings. The loud noises, the arguments, the smell of cooking food, the pedestrians and their constant battle with the short-fused drivers — it all becomes a kind of soft buzz in the background of daily life, and you, too, have learned to tune it out.

When you tune out the chatter, you find, there is so much about the city to love. There are your tucked-away corners with friends, places that you seem to have almost planted your flag in and claimed for yourself. There are familiar faces and quiet hideouts that provide a much-needed pause between the frenzied running around demanded by such an expansive urban layout. You are soon able to recognize almost every street corner and building front, intimately acquainted with the way everything works, able to help the waves of newcomers who shamefully analyze their map and GPS in the middle of the sidewalk. They're cute, you think — made all the more cute by the fact that you used to be them. You remember feeling so new, so scared, and then suddenly completely comfortable, inextricably involved with what you consider to be your city.

It is your city, you think. It's all of ours at once, every last local you pass on the street with a kind of understanding look of amused exasperation at the tourists. It's ours because we each have a slightly different version of it, a varying angle on an unfailingly beautiful view, and no one ever loves it in exactly the same way twice.

10

How To Say Goodbye To Someone You Don't Want To Leave

Over three years ago, I stayed with a friend in a new city, and his friends all came over and made steak tartare and fries for a welcome dinner. They became my first new friends. Since, I had never seen them all together in the same place, for constraints of time or distance or scheduling. Last night, we were all together again — every last one of us — and made steak tartare and fries as a goodbye dinner. It was the kind of farewell where you don't even really need to say anything, because part of you knows that it will happen again, it's just a question of when.

A few days earlier, I had endings that were much better-articulated.

"You're a really good person," I told a friend in the hallway of the house party, "and I'm really glad that I got to know you."

It was the last one we'd have just like that, with all of us in the same place and the same level of freedom and the same open future ahead of us. I would come back some day, yes, but nothing would be quite the same. And that's a good thing. It's always tinged with a certain sadness when groups of friends remain exactly the same over the course of a few years, but a selfish part of every person wants people to repeat themselves out of nostalgia. You want to put everything into a little music box and open it up at will, seeing the tiny dancers spinning just the way they were when you left them.

His cheeks flared red when I said this. We weren't, like most friends, used to speaking so candidly about the way we feel towards each other. He told me some sweet things, and I felt a catch at the back of my throat. "Don't cry," I thought, "It's going to be all weird if you cry, and tonight is about having fun."

There is no perfect way to execute a goodbye. There is the lightness and the familiarity that we all want, the feeling that even its final moments, a relationship is still just as fun as it always was. Because when we are saying goodbye to someone, we're not just talking to them, we're talking to the person that we are at this very moment. We know, even if we don't want to admit it, that we will never be in this exact same spot again. We will never see the world the same way, and closing the door on someone's chapter means committing it officially to memory — that it's no longer an organic, living thing.

"If nothing ever changes," we think, without even really thinking it, "then maybe we can be young forever."

I think I said a hundred goodbyes that night, sometimes forcing myself to go back and add one last thought before the person walked out the door. I told certain people what I've always thought of them, told them that I believed in them, told them that they were good at that thing they've always considered just a hobby. Goodbyes are a certain brush with mortality, the feeling of time running out that leads you to say every thing you've ever considered too uncomfortably honest. There were people I've known for years who only in that moment heard what I truly felt for them with no filter, and all I regretted was not having told them before.

There are people we will never be able to say goodbye to, even if we have to leave. They are the ones we will make every last effort to stay close to, the people we will write and call and video chat with in the early morning hours to accommodate time zone discrepancies. The two of you will look at ticket prices and plan trips and make sure there is always a couch that the other can crash on, even on short notice. They are the loves that can't be tempered by distance or time, and the goodbyes you force yourselves to say are really just an "I'll see you soon," even if they make your chest hurt in the moment. Even when you are about to leave, you imagine that you'll see them just one more time, even if it's getting a coffee at the airport terminal.

When the party was over, I wondered how many of these people I would really never see again. I picked up my belongings and walked as slowly as possible to the door, counting every step to see how long I could make the exit last. And while I knew, on some level, that many of the goodbyes I had said were permanent ones, I thought it better to assume that I would see all of them again some day, even in the same room. It seemed a better way to live life, imagining that your next reunion is just around the corner, and that your story will never have to come to a real ending.

11

10 Thoughts I Have While Packing To Move To New York (From Paris)

1. It always feels like saying goodbye to people is a living, breathing thing. The conversations you have where everything is urgent and final (and you say the things that are important and bittersweet) are too heavy to leave sitting on their own, bookending the time you spent together. You almost have to lighten it all with another coffee, another lunch, another couple of drinks on a terrace so everything can be regular and normal and not-sad again. No one ever wants to hug and cry and say those real, hard goodbyes. Maybe they make you feel a little better when you actually get on the plane — as though you have placed something in its final resting spot — but they always feel like they are going to kill you in the moment, like your heart is going to burst.

2. The amount of shit that we accumulate is just monstrous. Going through papers, receipts, old mail,

cards, it all feels like you're surrounded by a cloud of dust, like Pig-Pen in the Peanuts comics. How do we ever let ourselves be so well-documented? When we keep these little paper proofs of existence, do we really think that we'll ever need them again? I dedicated a folder just to the paper items that I want to take with me, make a collage of, and frame. How do I have so many train tickets? So many postcards that I never gave a proper thank you for? Eventually, the folder got too thick and threatened to compromise my relatively limited baggage space, and I started deciding what was and wasn't good enough to take with me. The first thing that had to stay was the ticket to the Brel concert I saw for my first birthday here. It changes colors when you move it in the light.

3. My French friends are always mythicizing New York, and the Americans are always fawning over Paris. Neither perspective seems particularly just or realistic (I'm assuming for New York, I have never lived there). But there is something pleasant about listening to them talk about it. When I walk through Paris with a friend who is visiting, everything is in Technicolor. Everything is just so interesting, so beautiful, so novel. When they ask me to talk about it, I feel like I'm telling them a fairy tale about a city that exists only in snippets from perfume commercials. And when my French friends talk about how much they want to go to New York, how big and fast and thrilling and young and cutting-edge it all is, I can't help but feel a twinge of pride. "Yes," I think, "Paris is

a beautiful little music box of a city. New York is going to be a jungle."

4. New York intimidates me immensely. While putting the little guidebooks and maps I got upon my arrival in Paris into the "Donate" box, I can't help but marvel at how compact it all is. It's a city of 40 square miles, compared to New York's 400-something. I could walk from my apartment in Saint Michel all the way to the south end of the city in a little over an hour. New York seems so enormous, so full of people and things that will never want to get to know you.

5. I have never tried escargot. I have been confronted with it so many times, and each time the prospect offends me in such a profound way that I can't bring myself to not be "that guy," that incredibly unadventurous and culturally-limited guy. It's just… the texture. The knowledge I have of what a snail is. I can't disconnect it from the inarguably luscious parsley butter. There are other things I've eaten so many times that I feel I'll never be able to get the taste out of my mouth. The bakery next to my old apartment made macarons so perfect — so crisp on the outside, chewy on the inside, and filled thick with cream — that I couldn't invite people over without getting a little box of them for everyone to try. Once, for breakfast, I went and got myself a box of six and made a big pot of tea. It might have been my best morning ever.

6. I miss good Chinese food. There are pockets here and there in Paris, but for the most part, the Chinese take-out options are fairly bleak. For every incredible

Szechuan hole-in-the-wall restaurant that makes you cry of simultaneous pleasure and pain, there are a thousand lackluster takeout joints that can't even do a good beef with broccoli. I miss the little boxes, the bag of crispy noodles, and the comfort of curling up under a blanket on the couch and watching a movie with your dinner. When I put a business card from my favorite takeout place into my "Collage" folder, I think about how it was still just something to order in a pinch. I can't wait for the kind of takeout Chinese you go out of your way for.

7. There is something so satisfying about the act of packing a suitcase. You can arrange, and rearrange, and re-rearrange, playing Tetris with your belongings until everything seems to be in the perfect order. I look over at my bags a lot and wonder how many more of them I would need if I didn't fold my dresses just so, or get rid of half of the things I wanted to take with me. There always comes the moment, though, when I feel like I could do it just that much better. I take everything out and start over again, and everything becomes refreshed and calm. It's a form of control that we rarely get.

8. There aren't really seasons in Paris, so to speak. There are clearly changes in general temperature, and there are leaves that come and go as they do anywhere. But "spring," "winter" and "fall" are less clearly-defined periods of weather and more long, blurry stretches of rain and grey that erode your ability to get your bearings. From dawn until late evening, the sky is a shade of grey that completely obscures the sun and

seems to be precariously close the ground. From September until May, there are variations in coldness, but there is always the same chilly, life-sapping rain. It's the part of Paris they rarely tell you about, the part where — like this spring — everyone is overcome with a kind of Seasonal Affective Disorder that turns every basic activity into a foot-dragging trial. By the time summer comes around, you are happy to melt under the sun and forgo air conditioning for a little bit of dry air. The sun on your skin feels like a strange, wonderful thing. It has snowed twice in the three years I've lived here, and one time it even stuck, for about a day. Just enough to bring all transport to a complete standstill.

9. I will miss the architecture. I have explored most of Williamsburg on Google Street View — as my memories from the four days I spent there in 2010 are rather vague — and it has its charm. It has a kind of style. But there is an industrial, necessary quality about it that makes everything look just a little too human. Parisian architecture is utter whipped cream, superfluous flakes of gold and wrought-iron curlicues and curving roofs and tiny little chimneys everywhere. The sprawling governmental buildings which, despite their very tedious functions, are remnants of monarchies who valued aesthetics above all else. You get your boring paperwork processed in 18th-century estates. Everything feels just a little better than it needs to be.

10. My friend asks me when I'm going to come back as I sort through my books, 90 percent of which I will

have to sell or give away. "I think in the spring, we will come back to visit friends and family. I hope." I don't tell her that every night I look at the ticket prices, and am already planning my next trip back before I have even left. I don't tell her that, no matter how wonderful New York will be and how highly my friends here speak of my future life there, I am terrified. I don't tell her that I am taking way too long to pack each bag, that I feel like I'm putting my sense of comfort and warmth into the "Donate" pile as I go, that I don't know if I will ever feel at home again.

About the Writer

Photograph by Ludovic Etienne

Chelsea is Senior Writer at Thought Catalog. She is also the author of *I'm Only Here for the WiFi*, *IRL Porn*, and *Take Out Your Earrings Before You Fight*. She lives in Brooklyn, and recently painted her kitchen a striking shade of navy blue.

THOUGHT
CATALOG
Books

Thought Catalog Books is a publishing house owned by The Thought & Expression Company, an independent media group based in Brooklyn, NY. Founded in 2010, we are committed to facilitating thought and expression. We exist to help people become better communicators and listeners in order to engender a more exciting, attentive, and imaginative world.

Visit us on the web at
www.thoughtcatalogbooks.com and *www.collective.world.*